MEGAN RAPINOE

SPORTS SUPERSTARS

BY GOLRIZ GOLKAR

BELLWETHER MEDIA · MINNEAPOLIS, MN

Torque brims with excitement perfect for thrill-seekers of all kinds. Discover daring survival skills, explore uncharted worlds, and marvel at mighty engines and extreme sports. In *Torque* books, anything can happen. Are you ready?

This edition first published in 2024 by Bellwether Media, Inc.

No part of this publication may be reproduced in whole or in part without written permission of the publisher. For information regarding permission, write to Bellwether Media, Inc., Attention: Permissions Department, 6012 Blue Circle Drive, Minnetonka, MN 55343.

Library of Congress Cataloging-in-Publication Data

LC record for Megan Rapinoe available at: https://lccn.loc.gov/2023040022

Text copyright © 2024 by Bellwether Media, Inc. TORQUE and associated logos are trademarks and/or registered trademarks of Bellwether Media, Inc.

Editor: Rebecca Sabelko   Designer: Gabriel Hilger

Printed in the United States of America, North Mankato, MN.

TABLE OF CONTENTS

ROAD TO GOLD 4
WHO IS MEGAN RAPINOE? 6
A RISING STAR 8
A STAR ON THE SOCCER FIELD 12
A SOCCER SUPERSTAR 20
GLOSSARY 22
TO LEARN MORE 23
INDEX 24

ROAD TO GOLD

It is the women's soccer **semifinals** at the 2012 London **Summer Olympics**. Canada is leading 2–1 over the United States.

Megan Rapinoe has an open shot to the **goal** for the U.S. She shoots the ball into the net like a rocket. The U.S. wins the game 4–3. They go to the **finals**!

Fun on the Field

Rapinoe would celebrate goals in fun ways. She often stretched her arms out wide when her team scored. She once sang into a microphone after scoring a goal!

WHO IS MEGAN RAPINOE?

Megan Rapinoe is a former **professional** soccer player. She played **forward**. She was a top scorer on the U.S. Women's National Soccer Team (USWNT). She helped the team win **Women's World Cups** and Olympic medals. Rapinoe also played in the **National Women's Soccer League** (NWSL).

Equal Rights

In 2016, some athletes kneeled during the national anthem before games. They were showing that they disagreed with the inequality Black people face. Rapinoe also kneeled to show her support.

MEGAN RAPINOE

BIRTHDAY	July 5, 1985
HOMETOWN	Redding, California
POSITION	forward
HEIGHT	5 feet 7 inches
DRAFTED	Chicago Red Stars in the 1st round (2nd overall) of the 2009 Women's Professional Soccer (WPS) Draft

Rapinoe fights for gender and racial equality.

7

A RISING STAR

Around age 5, Rapinoe and her twin sister began playing soccer. They were both strong players. Rapinoe stood out. At age 16, she was chosen to play on the U.S. Soccer Under-17 youth team.

RAPINOE WITH HER PARENTS

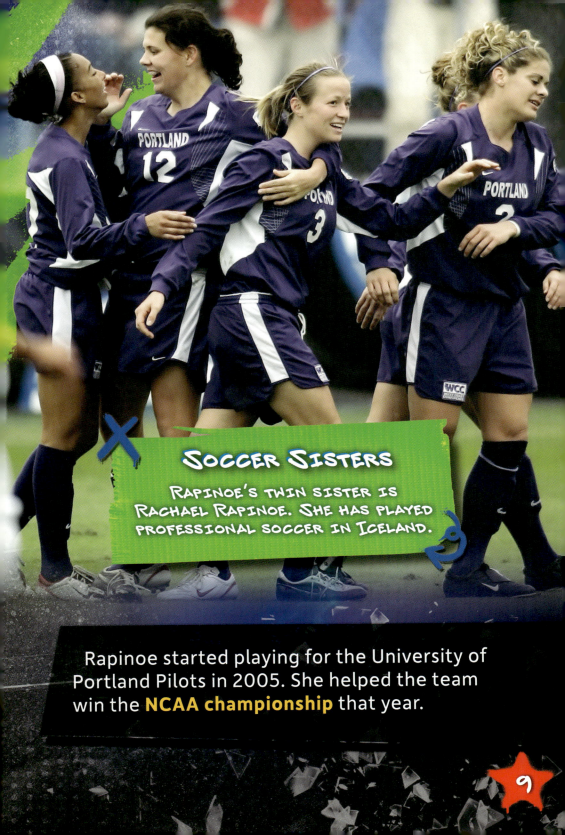

Soccer Sisters

Rapinoe's twin sister is Rachael Rapinoe. She has played professional soccer in Iceland.

Rapinoe started playing for the University of Portland Pilots in 2005. She helped the team win the **NCAA championship** that year.

Rapinoe joined the USWNT during her second year with the Pilots. But she hurt her knee that fall. She could not play for much of two seasons.

Rapinoe was ready to play for her last season with the Pilots. She was a top scorer. Professional teams wanted her to play for them. In 2009, she joined the Chicago Red Stars.

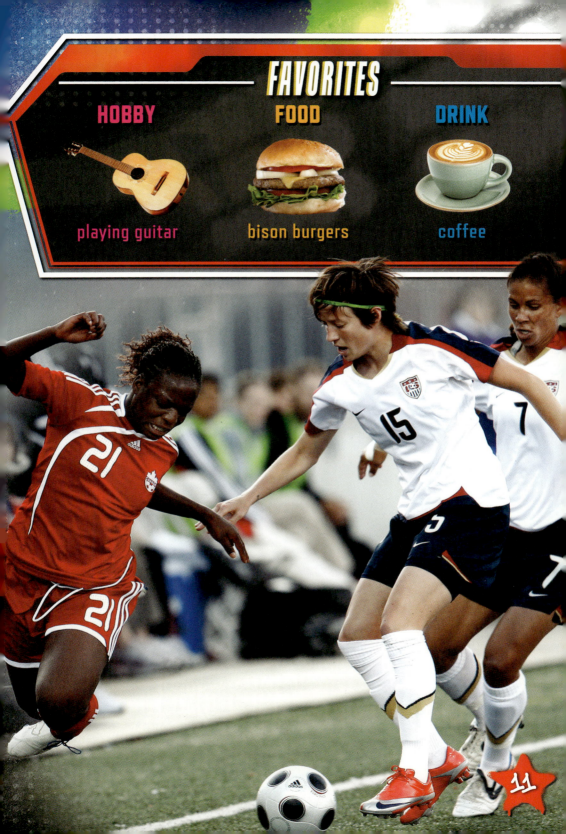

A STAR ON THE SOCCER FIELD

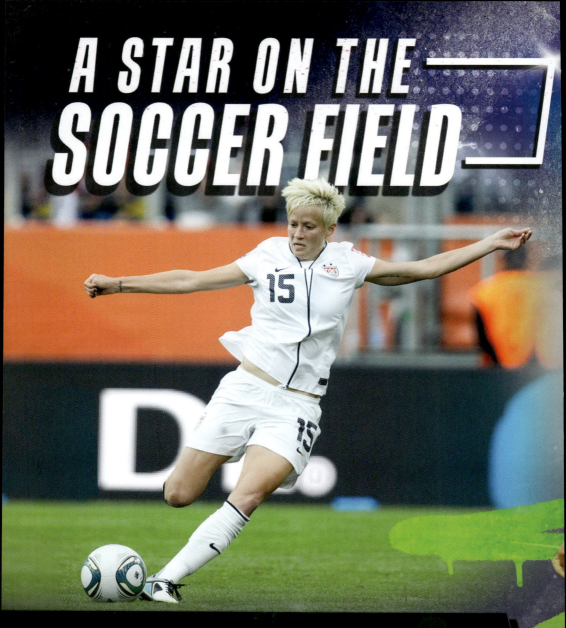

Rapinoe was a top player for the Red Stars. But the team split up in 2010. She was a standout player for other teams until the women's professional league ended in early 2012.

12

Rapinoe also kept playing for the USWNT. In 2011, she played in her first Women's World Cup. The team lost in the final.

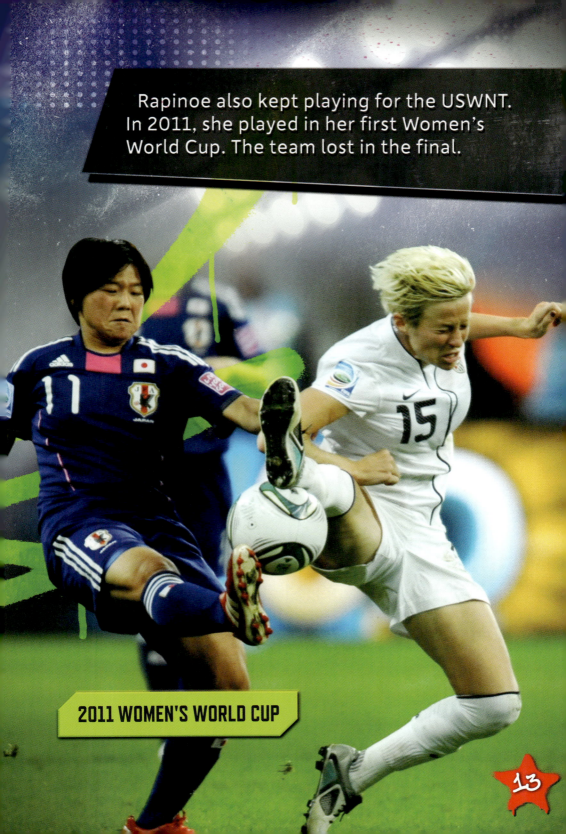

2011 WOMEN'S WORLD CUP

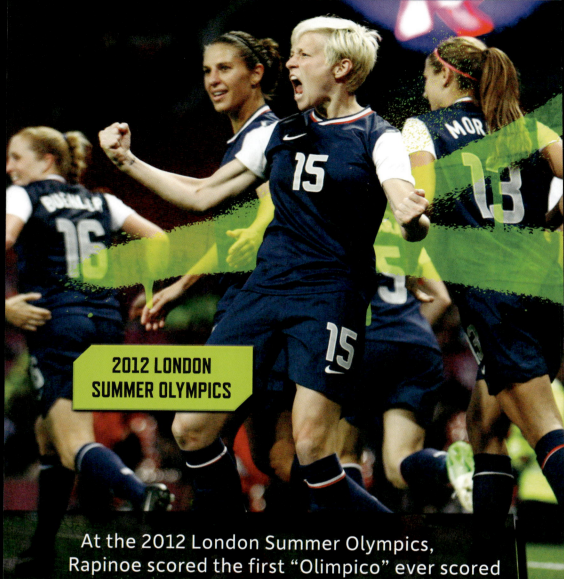

2012 LONDON SUMMER OLYMPICS

At the 2012 London Summer Olympics, Rapinoe scored the first "Olimpico" ever scored at an Olympic Games. She scored the goal on a kick from the corner of the soccer field! Rapinoe helped Team USA win the gold medal.

Rapinoe spent 2013 playing for Olympique Lyonnais in France. She helped the team win league titles.

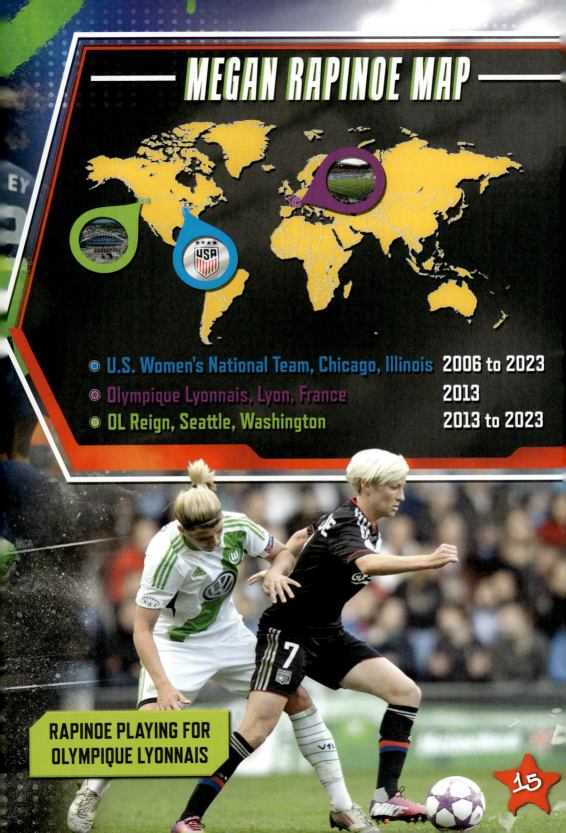

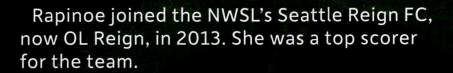

Rapinoe joined the NWSL's Seattle Reign FC, now OL Reign, in 2013. She was a top scorer for the team.

In 2015, Rapinoe played in another World Cup. The team won! She started training for the 2016 Rio de Janeiro Summer Olympics soon after the World Cup. But she hurt her knee during a practice. She did not play much during the Olympics.

RAPINOE PLAYING FOR SEATTLE REIGN FC IN 2013

2015 WORLD CUP CHAMPIONS

TROPHY SHELF

FIFA Women's World Cup champion

FIFA Women's Player of the Year

2-time Olympic medalist

Ballon d'Or winner

17

Rapinoe scored many goals for OL Reign in 2017. In 2018, she broke a USWNT record with four **assists** in a single game.

Rapinoe led the USWNT to a second World Cup win in 2019. She became the **FIFA** Women's Player of the Year. She also won the Ballon d'Or. It named her the best female soccer player in the world for that year!

TIMELINE

— 2009 —
Rapinoe is drafted by the Red Stars

— 2012 —
Rapinoe wins an Olympic gold medal

— 2013 —
Rapinoe joins Seattle Reign, now called OL Reign

2019 WOMEN'S WORLD CUP

— 2015 —
Rapinoe wins her first World Cup championship

— 2019 —
Rapinoe wins her second World Cup championship and a Ballon d'Or award

— 2022 —
Rapinoe is awarded the Presidential Medal of Freedom

A SOCCER SUPERSTAR

Rapinoe has worked hard for equal rights. In 2022, she received the Presidential Medal of Freedom. She was honored for her fight for equality in women's sports.

PRESIDENTIAL MEDAL OF FREEDOM

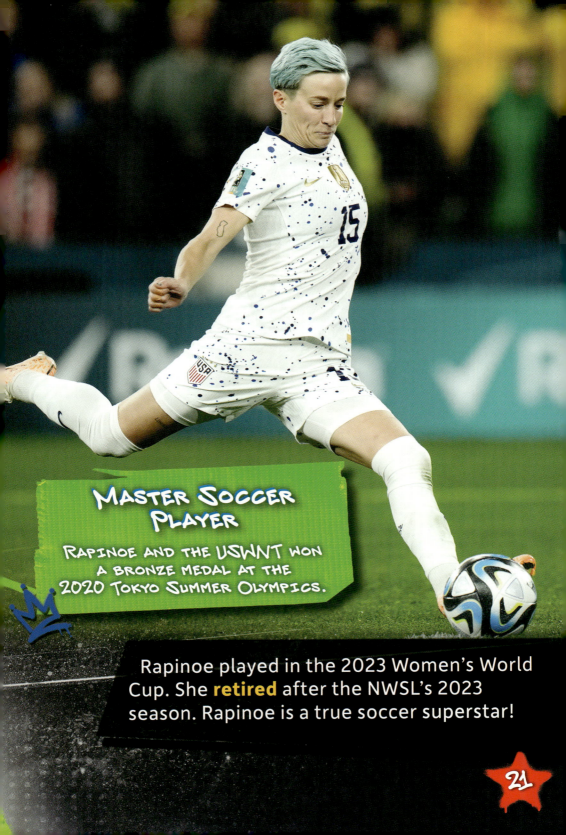

Master Soccer Player

Rapinoe and the USWNT won a bronze medal at the 2020 Tokyo Summer Olympics.

Rapinoe played in the 2023 Women's World Cup. She **retired** after the NWSL's 2023 season. Rapinoe is a true soccer superstar!

GLOSSARY

assists—passes to teammates that result in goals

FIFA—an international association that oversees soccer and two other related sports; FIFA stands for International Federation of Association Football.

finals—the championship series of a sports tournament

forward—a position in soccer that involves trying to score or help teammates score goals

goal—either net on a soccer field that players shoot the ball into to score a point; points in soccer are also called goals.

National Women's Soccer League—a professional women's soccer league at the top of the U.S. soccer league system

NCAA championship—a contest held every year by the National Collegiate Athletic Association, or NCAA, that decides the best college team or person

professional—related to a player, team, or coach who makes money from a sport

retired—stopped working, or stopped playing a sport professionally

semifinals—the series of games played to determine which teams play in the final series of a sports tournament

Summer Olympics—a worldwide summer sports contest held in a different country every four years

Women's World Cups—international soccer competitions held every four years; the Women's World Cup is the world's largest women's soccer tournament.

TO LEARN MORE

AT THE LIBRARY

Chandler, Matt. *Megan Rapinoe: World Cup Champion.* North Mankato, Minn.: Capstone Press, 2021.

Fishman, Jon M. *Megan Rapinoe.* Minneapolis, Minn.: Lerner Publications, 2021.

Scarbrough, Mary Hertz. *Megan Rapinoe.* Greensboro, N.C.: Rourke Publishing, 2021.

ON THE WEB

Factsurfer.com gives you a safe, fun way to find more information.

1. Go to www.factsurfer.com

2. Enter "Megan Rapinoe" into the search box and click 🔍.

3. Select your book cover to see a list of related content.

INDEX

assists, 18
awards, 14, 17, 18, 20, 21
Ballon d'Or, 18
Chicago Red Stars, 10, 12
childhood, 8
equality, 6, 7, 20
family, 8, 9
favorites, 11
FIFA Women's Player of the Year, 18
finals, 4, 13
forward, 6
goal, 4, 14, 18
injury, 10, 16
map, 15
National Women's Soccer League, 6, 16, 21
NCAA championship, 9
OL Reign, 16, 18
Olimpico, 14
Olympique Lyonnais, 14, 15
Presidential Medal of Freedom, 20
profile, 7
record, 18
retired, 21
scorer, 6, 10, 16
Summer Olympics, 4, 6, 14, 16, 21
timeline, 18–19
trophy shelf, 17
University of Portland Pilots, 9, 10
U.S. Soccer Under-17 team, 8
U.S. Women's National Soccer Team, 4, 6, 10, 13, 14, 18, 21
World Cup, 6, 13, 16, 17, 18, 19, 21

The images in this book are reproduced through the courtesy of: Shaina Benhiyoun/SPP/ AP Images/ AP Newsroom, front cover; lev radin, pp. 3, 17; Hussein Malla/ AP Images/ AP Newsroom, pp. 4, 6; Action Plus Sports Images/ Alamy, pp. 4-5; Kim Price/ AP Images/ AP Newsroom, p. 7 (Megan Rapinoe); ZUMA Press/ Alamy, p. 8; David J. Phillip/ AP Images/ AP Newsroom, p. 9; Jae C. Hong/ AP Images/ AP Newsroom, p. 10; uncepepin, p. 11 (guitar); images.etc., p. 11 (bison burger); Visit Roemvanitch, p. 11 (coffee); Nathan Denette/ AP Images/ AP Newsroom, p. 11 (Megan Rapinoe); dpa picture alliance/ Alamy, pp. 12, 13, 15 (Megan Rapinoe); David Moir/ Reuters, p. 14; Grindstone Media Group, p. 15 (OL Reign stadium); katatonia82, p. 15 (Olympique Lyonnais stadium); Alan Schwartz/ AP Images/ AP Newsroom, p. 16; Romain Biard, p. 18 (Megan Rapinoe); Chicago Red Stars/ Wiki Commons, p. 18 (Chicago Red Stars logo); Tony Baggett, p. 18 (Olympic gold medal); OL Reign/ Wiki Commons, p. 18 (OL Reign logo); Francisco Seco/ AP Images/ AP Newsroom, p. 19 (2019 Women's World Cup); PA Images/ Alamy, p. 19 (World Cup Championship trophy); Orange Pics BV/ Alamy, p. 19 (Megan Rapinoe with World Cup trophy); J. Scott Applewhite/ AP Images/ AP Newsroom, p. 20; Jose Breton/ AP Images/ AP Newsroom, p. 21; feelphoto, p. 23.